Dinosaurs

Carnotaurus

by Julie Murray

Dash!
LEVELED READERS
An Imprint of Abdo Zoom • abdobooks.com

Dash!
LEVELED READERS

Level 1 – Beginning
Short and simple sentences with familiar words or patterns for children who are beginning to understand how letters and sounds go together.

Level 2 – Emerging
Longer words and sentences with more complex language patterns for readers who are practicing common words and letter sounds.

Level 3 – Transitional
More developed language and vocabulary for readers who are becoming more independent.

THIS BOOK CONTAINS RECYCLED MATERIALS

abdobooks.com

Published by Abdo Zoom, a division of ABDO, PO Box 398166, Minneapolis, Minnesota 55439.

Printed in the United States of America, North Mankato, Minnesota.
052024
092024

Photo Credits: Alamy, Shutterstock
Production Contributors: Kenny Abdo, Jennie Forsberg, Grace Hansen, John Hansen
Design Contributors: Neil Klinepier

Library of Congress Control Number: 2023948503

Publisher's Cataloging in Publication Data

Names: Murray, Julie, author.
Title: Carnotaurus / by Julie Murray
Description: Minneapolis, Minnesota : Abdo Zoom, 2025 | Series: Dinosaurs | Includes online resources and index.
Identifiers: ISBN 9781098285425 (lib. bdg.) | ISBN 9781098286125 (ebook) | ISBN 9781098286477 (Read-to-me eBook)
Subjects: LCSH: Dinosaurs--Juvenile literature. | Carnotaurus--Juvenile literature. | Prehistoric animals--Juvenile literature. | Paleontology--Juvenile literature. | Extinct animals--Juvenile literature.
Classification: DDC 567.9--dc23

Table of Contents

Carnotaurus

Carnotaurus was a **theropod** dinosaur. It lived 70 million years ago!

Carnotaurus lived in what is South America today. It was found in wetlands and plains.

It could grow up to 30 feet (9.1 m) long. It weighed up to 3,000 pounds (1,360 kg).

Carnotaurus had a large body. Its skin was lined in rows of cone-shaped bumps.

It walked on two powerful legs. It had two tiny arms. The arms were likely useless.

The tail made up 13 feet (3.96 m) of the dinosaur's length. It helped with balance.

Carnotaurus had a six inch (15.2 cm) horn above each eye.

Carnotaurus was a **carnivore**. It mainly ate small animals. But it also ate larger dinosaurs!

The first Carnotaurus **fossils** were discovered in Argentina. José Bonaparte **excavated** them in 1984.

More Facts

- *Carnotaurus* means "meat-eating bull." It is named for what it ate and its bull-like head.

- It was a fast dinosaur. It could run over 20 miles per hour (32 kph).

- Only one set of **fossils** have been found! The findings included **impressions** of the dinosaur's skin.

Glossary

carnivore – an animal that only eats meat.

excavated – uncovered by digging.

fossil – the remains or trace of a living animal or plant from a long time ago. Fossils are found embedded in earth or rock.

impression – a mark made by pressing.

theropod – any dinosaur of the suborder Theropoda, such as Tyrannosaurus rex and velociraptor, characterized by hollow bones and three-toed limbs, usually possessing short forelimbs and walking on two legs.

Index

Online Resources

Booklinks
NONFICTION NETWORK
FREE! ONLINE NONFICTION RESOURCES

To learn more about Carnotaurus, please visit **abdobooklinks.com** or scan this QR code. These links are routinely monitored and updated to provide the most current information available.